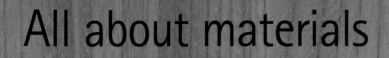

Is it hard?
All about solids

Jenny Vaughan
Experiments by Meredith Blakeney

FRANKLIN WATTS
LONDON • SYDNEY

First published in 2009
by Franklin Watts

Copyright © Franklin Watts 2009

Franklin Watts
338 Euston Road
London NW1 3BH

Franklin Watts Australia
Level 17/207 Kent Street
Sydney, NSW 2000

Series editor: Sarah Peutrill
Art director: Jonathan Hair
Design: Elaine Wilkinson
Photographs: Paul Bricknell (unless otherwise credited)

Picture credits: Shutterstock: pp 4t (David P. Smith), 4bl (Daniel
Goodings), 4br (niderlander), 5 (Laura Litman), 6 (Sebastian Duda), 7l
(sajko), 7r, 10 (Neil Roy Johnson), 11t (Jasenka Luksa), 12t (Maksym
Gorpenyuk), 12b (Jakez), 13 (Stuart Miles), 14l (Galyna Andrushko),
14r (tatiana sayig), 15t (Sharon Meredith), 16t (Ragne Kabanova), 16b
(Ragne Kabanova), 17t (Dean Evangelista), 17b (JoLin), 20 (Jonathan
Vasata), 21t (Multiart), 22 (Leon Chong), 23t (William Attard
McCarthy), 26t (Filipchuk Oleg Vasiliovich), 26b (Laurence Gough), 27
(Michael J Thompson); Wishlist Images: 8, 9, 21b.
Cover images: Shutterstock: br (Laura Litman), tl (Volodymyr
Kyrylyuk), tr (Neil Roy Johnson)

With thanks to our models: Conah Caple, Mary Conquest, Katie Lloyd,
Chris Penny, Darnell Smith.

Dewey number: 530.4

ISBN 978 0 7496 8718 2

Printed in China

Franklin Watts is a division of Hachette Children's Books, an Hachette
UK company.

www.hachette.co.uk

Please note: The investigations in this book have been thoroughly
checked and tested. We regret that the Author and Publisher cannot
be held responsible for any accidents or injury incurred while
following them.

Contents

The topics highlighted above are investigations you can try.

Words in bold are in the glossary on page 30.

What is a solid?

A **solid** is a **material** that has a definite shape, which does not easily change. Because of this, we can make solids into useful objects, such as furniture, cars and much, much more.

Trees are made of solid wood, which we can cut and shape – like the planks the house is made from.

'States of matter'

Most materials that are solids can come in other forms, too. These forms are called '**states of matter**'. For example, water can be solid ice, liquid and even a gas, called water vapour. Liquids, except when they are tiny drops, have no shape of their own – they take the shape of whatever container they are in, though they may not always fill it. Gases, too, have no shape, and they can spread out to fill the container they are in.

Liquids, like this orange juice, take the shape of their container.

We cannot normally see most gases. We can only see this natural gas because it is burning.

Different kinds of solids

Solids can be very different from each other. They have different **characteristics**. They can be weak and easy to break, or very **strong**. They can be squashy, or bendy, stiff and hard, easy or difficult to scratch, or stretchy or not. The way we use different solids depends on their characteristics.

Humans change and treat solids in many ways to make useful things – such as cars and buildings. What else can you see that is solid in this picture?

What is 'hardness'?

A solid is **hard** when it is not fluffy or squashy like a cushion or a blanket. But 'hardness' can have another important meaning, too, describing how difficult a material is to cut or scratch.

Scratching solids

Materials that seem to be alike may vary in this kind of hardness. For example, steel is hard, and much more difficult to scratch than metals such as gold or aluminium. Some rocks, such as flint, are very hard, while others are much softer and can easily be carved, scratched or worn away. Some kinds of wood are harder than others, too. Of all the solids that are found naturally, diamonds are the most difficult to cut or scratch.

Diamonds are an extremely hard form of a material called carbon.

Sharp edges

The kinds of hard materials that are difficult to scratch are useful for scratching and cutting other materials. They can be made into sharp knives and pointed blades. This is why prehistoric people chose flint to make arrowheads and knives.

The stonemason uses a hard metal blade to cut softer stone.

Find a solid object, such as a coin. Is it hard or soft? Is it hard in some ways and not others?

Scratching surfaces

You will need:

A large nail, a plastic knife or fork, a wooden cocktail stick, a sharp stone. Surfaces to test, such as: an old saucepan, the plastic lid from a yoghurt pot, a stone, a piece of wood.

Scientists have a scale to show how difficult it is to scratch different substances. It is called a 'scale of hardness'. If you can scratch one material with another, the one that does the scratching is higher up the scale. Diamonds are at the top of the scale, as almost nothing can scratch them.

Try scratching the saucepan with the plastic knife, the cocktail stick, the stone and the nail. Will any of them make a scratch? If they can, they are harder than the pan.

Try scratching the wood with the nail, the plastic knife and the stone. Are all the scratchers harder than the wood? Do the same with the plastic lid.

1

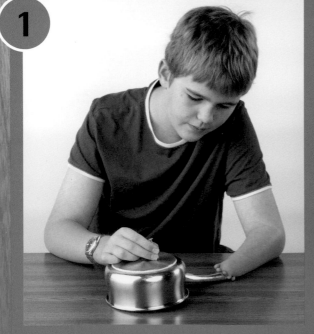

2

Try scratching the stone with the nail, the wooden cocktail stick and the plastic knife. Are any of the scratchers harder than the stone?

3

WARNING:
This experiment uses sharp objects. Make sure there is an adult with you when you try it.

Do some more tests

Try testing with other 'scratchers' and other materials. For example, find out which is harder – your fingernail or a bar of soap? Can you find any scratcher that will make a mark on an old mirror?

Hard and sharp

Tools for cutting and **drilling** need very thin edges or fine points that can cut other materials easily. If they are made from a hard material, these tools can cut without quickly wearing out and becoming blunt.

Sharpening

To sharpen blunt tools, we make the edge thin by rubbing away on either side of it. The best cutting tools are hard enough to stay sharp for a long time, but soft enough to sharpen.

Hard, sharp metal tools cut and shape softer wood and stone.

Scouring and sanding

Hard materials are also useful for scraping away softer ones. For example, **carpenters** use sandpaper (tiny pieces of hard glass stuck to paper) to smooth rough surfaces on wood, or get rid of paint. Cooks use metal or even plastic scourers to scrape burnt food from saucepans.

Sandpaper makes the rough surface of wood smooth.

Many pencils are marked to show how hard the **graphite** (the black part in the middle) in them is. H means hard, and B means soft. So 4H is very hard, and 4B very soft. HB is in-between. How long does a 4H pencil stay sharp? Does a 4B pencil stay sharp for as long?

Shaping solids

Cutting and carving are not the only ways in which we can alter the shape of a solid. Some are **malleable**. This means we can beat or push them into different shapes without breaking them.

Wet and squashy

Damp clay is malleable. All over the world, people shape it to make things, such as pots, bricks or even houses. When it is dry, it is hard and is no longer malleable – unless water is added to it again. This is a **reversible** change. If the clay is baked in a very hot oven, it changes completely. It becomes harder and cannot return to being malleable. This is an **irreversible** change. The bricks and tiles used to make modern houses, and china cups and plates are made from baked clay.

A potter makes a vase from malleable clay, then bakes it until it is hard.

Mud buildings last well in dry places. Elsewhere, they must be protected from the rain, or the mud will wash away.

Making materials malleable

Some materials become malleable if they are heated. These include wax, glass and chocolate. Metals are malleable. Some are malleable all the time. Other metals, such as steel, have to be heated, or be in very thin sheets or strands before they can be bent or shaped.

Try shaping modelling clay and let it dry out. What happens if you try to bend it after it is dry? Why do you think modelling clay is often sold in air-tight containers?

Strength

We say a solid is strong if it can be pulled, bent or squashed and pressed without breaking. Being strong is not the same as being hard. Rope, for example, is soft – but it can be strong.

Is it easy to break?

Glass is hard but not strong. If we try to bend it or hit it, it will shatter into pieces. (Do not try this, as sharp glass is dangerous.) Steel is stronger, and will not break.

This rope is strong enough to support the weight of a climber.

Glass breaks easily if we drop it or hit it.

Concrete block

Steel bar

Reinforcing concrete with steel gives it extra strength.

Making materials stronger

When we need to use a material, we choose one that is best for what we want to do with it. Sometimes, we alter materials to make them suit our needs better, or use several materials together. For example solid concrete is strong in some ways. It will not easily break if it is pushed or pressed. But it may break if it is bent or stretched. So, when concrete is used for building, a skeleton of steel is used to give the building extra strength. This is called **reinforcing** it.

Compare the strength of different materials. For example, which tears most easily – toilet paper or writing paper? Which breaks most easily – cotton thread or string? Which will bend without breaking – cardboard or a biscuit?

Letting light through

If we can see clearly through a material, we say it is **transparent**. If we can see light through it but we cannot see objects clearly, we say it is **translucent**. Materials that light cannot pass through are **opaque**.

The plain glass in a window lets plenty of light into a room.

Transparent solids

Many liquids are transparent, but not many solids. Those that are include thin sheets of ice, some plastics and glass. Glass is one of the most useful of all transparent solids. People have used it for hundreds of years in windows and the lenses of glasses, **telescopes** and **microscopes**. We can colour transparent materials – so that, when we look through them, everything seems to be coloured too. We can darken them, so everything seems darker when we look through them – for example, with sunglasses.

'Stained glass' windows allow only light of certain colours to pass through them.

Translucent materials

If we try looking through translucent materials, everything seems foggy. All we see are shapes and shadows. **Frosted glass** is translucent. It is often used for bathroom windows. You can test if a material is translucent. Try shining a torch through paper, and then card. You cannot see clearly through the paper. But if you can see light, it is translucent.

Translucent glass is useful for bathroom windows, because it lets light into the room, but no one can see you in there clearly.

These plastic tunnels let light through to the plants but you cannot see through them. They are translucent, not transparent.

Stained glass window

Stained glass is made by adding chemicals to melted glass, and then letting it cool and harden. You can make your own 'stained glass' using coloured boiled sweets.

You will need:

A packet of ready-made short-crust pastry, some flour, a rolling pin, cookie cutters of different sizes and shapes, cocktail stick, non-stick baking paper and a baking tray, oven gloves, knife, clear coloured boiled sweets, polythene freezer bags (the kind that zip up are best), cotton thread, a large needle.

Ask an adult to set the oven to 180°C/350°F/Gas Mark 4. Line a baking tray with non-stick baking paper. Roll out a sheet of pastry. Use the cookie cutters to make pastry shapes. Cut a round hole in each shape, around 2.5 cm across. Using a cocktail stick, make a small hole near the top of each one.

1

Place the shapes on the lined tray, and bake for 8 to 10 minutes.

Meanwhile, put the boiled sweets in polythene bags (one colour per bag) and hit them with the rolling pin until they are broken into small pieces. (You may need to ask an adult to help you.)

2

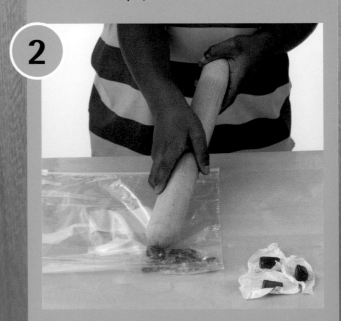

After around two minutes, the sweets will melt and fill the larger holes in the pastry. Let the 'windows' cool before you touch them. Then, with a large needle, gently push thread through the small hole at the top.

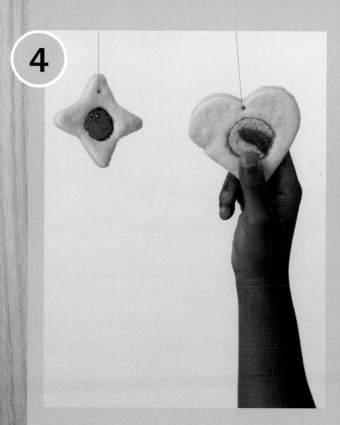

4

Use the thread to hang your 'stained glass' in front of a window, so the light can shine through it.

TAKE CARE:

This experiment uses a hot oven, and hot sugar. Both can be dangerous, so make sure you have an adult with you to help you.

What would happen?

Try putting two or more colours in one hole. What happens?

Solids that flow

Some solids, such as sand, sugar, **salt** and flour, are in the form of **grains** and **powders**. When we pour any of these into a container, they flow and seem to take its shape – as if they are liquids. Can we really say they are solids?

Tiny shapes

The answer is 'yes'. Each single grain or speck of powder is a tiny solid, which does not change its shape to fit the container. When they are tipped out onto a surface, they will usually remain in a heap, and do not flow away like a liquid. With larger grains, such as sand or sugar, we can even pick up one or two with our fingers.

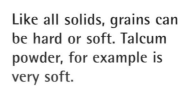

Like all solids, grains can be hard or soft. Talcum powder, for example is very soft.

Easy to move

The easiest way to move millions of grains at once is to carry them in a container – like a liquid. That is why you may sometimes see a tanker carrying sugar or flour, and why cooks sometimes measure out grains using cups and spoons – just like liquids.

This cook is using a measuring cup to measure small grains of crushed nuts.

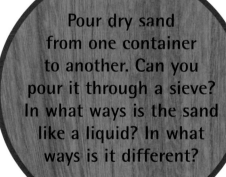

Pour dry sand from one container to another. Can you pour it through a sieve? In what ways is the sand like a liquid? In what ways is it different?

Disappearing solids

Some solids, such as sugar and salt, seem to vanish when we mix them with water. In fact, they have not disappeared, but have broken down into tiny particles in the water. They have **dissolved** in the water.

Seeing dissolved solids

Some solids dissolve, but can still be seen. Instant coffee, for example, colours water dark brown. Other solids do not dissolve, but tiny particles of them hang in a liquid, making it translucent or even opaque. This is what happens when you mix milk powder in water. The solids are **suspended** in the water.

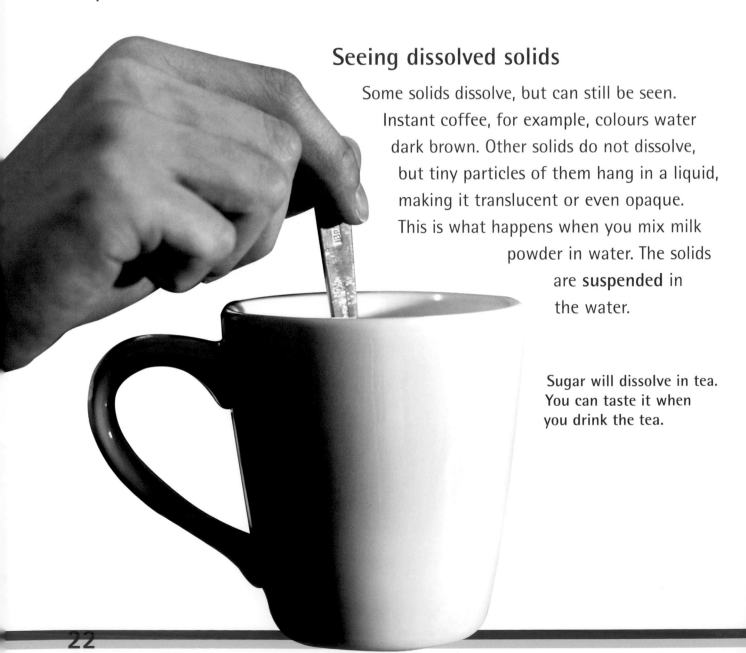

Sugar will dissolve in tea. You can taste it when you drink the tea.

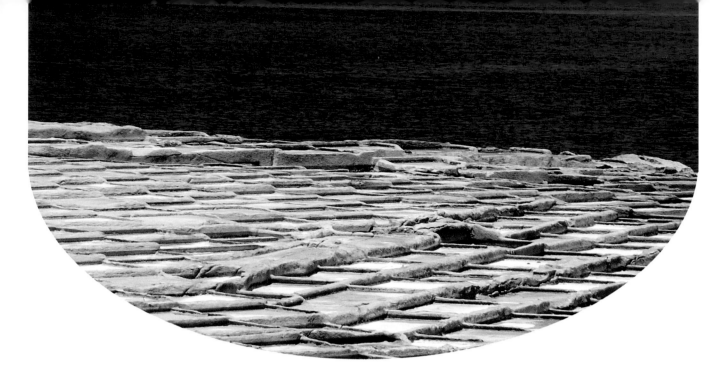

Evaporation

When a solid has dissolved or become suspended in water, we can get it back by letting the water **evaporate**. When water evaporates, it changes from being a liquid to a kind of gas, called water vapour. Any solids that were dissolved in it are left behind. Seawater has salt dissolved in it. This can be collected by trapping the water in pools. The water evaporates, leaving the salt behind.

As these pools of seawater evaporate, salt is left behind. This can be sold.

Test some solids to see if they will dissolve in water. Try sugar, salt and sand. Which ones will dissolve?

Invisible ink

You can use salt dissolved in water to make invisible ink. Make a simple design on paper with the salty water. When the water evaporates, it leaves behind a thin coating of hard salt. You can see this by rubbing a soft pencil over it.

You will need:

A spoon, two tablespoons of salt, two tablespoons of warm water, a jar, a paint-brush, plain white paper, a hairdryer, a soft pencil (e.g 4B), a hard pencil (e.g. 4H).

Mix two tablespoons of salt gradually with the same amount of warm water. Stir until as much salt has dissolved as possible.

With a paint-brush, use the salt-water to paint your initials or a simple design on the paper.

1

2

24

Dry the paper with a hairdryer.
What happens to your design?

Rub over the paper gently with the
side of the soft pencil. What can you
see now?

3

4

What would happen?

What happens if you rub the
design away with your fingers?
Can you remove it? Try the experiment again,
using a harder pencil. What happens?

Eaten away

Some solids will not dissolve in water, but will disappear when mixed with some chemicals, such as **acids**. This is not like salt dissolving in water. When a solid dissolves in an acid, it is changed into other substances.

Strong acids

Some acids are strong (powerful). These can be used to 'etch' or burn away patterns in solids such as metal. This process is sometimes used in making **circuit boards** for computers or other electronic equipment. Strong acids are dangerous and can injure us.

The circuit on a printed circuit board (PCB) can be made by etching away parts of a layer of metal on the board.

Weak acids

Weak acids are far less dangerous. Some, such as vinegar and lemon juice, are used in cooking. But even these can be painful if we get one in a cut, or in our eyes.

Gases in the air can form weak acids when they mix with rain. This is called **acid rain**. Over time, it can eat away at solid stone buildings and carvings.

Acid rain has eaten away at this stone building.

Stalagmites and stalactites

Air contains a gas called **carbon dioxide**. Mixed with water, carbon dioxide forms a weak acid. It drips through underground rocks, slowly dissolving them, to form caves. Water containing dissolved rock drips through the cave roof. As it does so, the acid changes back into plain water, carbon dioxide and solids from the dissolved rock. These build up into strange shapes, called stalagmites and stalactites.

Stalactites hang from the ceilings of caves. Stalagmites point up from the floor.

Vanishing eggshell

Vinegar is a weak acid – but it is strong enough to dissolve some solids. You can use vinegar to make an eggshell vanish.

First, take a whole raw egg and place it very gently in a glass jar or jug. Cover it with clear vinegar.

Can you see bubbles forming on the shell? Leave the shell in the jar for 24 hours. Check it every now and again, to see what you can observe.

What happens?

What do you notice about the
egg when you pour the vinegar away?

Glossary

acid A type of chemical that has a sour or sharp taste. Many acids will eat into hard substances.

acid rain Rain that has become acidic by mixing with certain gases in the air.

calcium carbonate A kind of solid that is found in bones, teeth and eggshells, and the rocks chalk, marble and limestone.

carbon dioxide A kind of gas found in the air.

carpenter Someone who makes buildings, furniture and so on, with wood.

characteristic Something that makes something special and different.

circuit board A board with a metal pathway along which electricity can flow. Circuit boards are found in computers and other electronic equipment.

dissolve We say a substance has dissolved when it turns into a liquid when we put it in another liquid.

drilling Making a hole with a machine called a drill.

etch To cut or burn a design on to a surface.

evaporate Change from liquid to gas.

frosted glass Glass that has been treated to make it look as if it is covered with frost – it allows light to pass through it, but we cannot see through it.

grains Small solid lumps, such as sand.

graphite The black material in the middle of pencils.

hard Difficult to cut or scratch.

irreversible A change that cannot be undone.

malleable Easy to press into different shapes without breaking.

material What something is made of.

melting Turning from solid to liquid after heating.

microscope An instrument that makes tiny things look larger.

opaque Opaque materials do not allow any light to pass through them.

powder Extremely small solid lumps (smaller than grains).

reinforcing Making stronger.

reversible A change than can be undone.

salt A chemical powder – we usually mean one particular kind of salt that we use for flavouring food, but there are many different salts.

solid A material which has a definite shape that does not easily change.

stained glass Glass that has been coloured with chemicals.

state of matter Whether matter (material) is solid, liquid or gas.

strong Not easy to break.

suspended When small particles of a solid hang in a liquid.

telescope An instrument for making distant objects, such as stars, appear nearer.

translucent A translucent material allows light to pass through it, but we cannot see clearly through it.

transparent Something we can see through.

Some answers

Page 5: In the picture, you can see: buildings, roads, road sign, cars, lorries, lamp-posts, walls, pillars supporting the road, air conditioning-unit on a flat roof, trees, grass.

Page 7: The coin is not squashy, so it is hard in one way. But it is softer than any substance that will make a scratch on its surface.

Page 9: A fingernail is a lot harder than soap. Few things are hard enough to scratch the mirror, but sandpaper, or the emery boards people use to file their nails, can make a faint mark.

Page 13: Modelling clay is sold in air-tight containers so that it does not dry out and stop being malleable.

Page 15: Toilet paper tears more easily than writing paper; cardboard will usually bend without breaking – but a biscuit won't.

Page 19: When you have two colours of sweets in some holes, they may run into each other where the colours meet. Use a strip of pastry to keep them separate.

Page 21: The sand will pour like a liquid, and it will pass easily through a sieve, as some liquids, such as water, will. The main way it is different from a liquid is that you can build it up into a heap, and it will stay there.

Page 23: Sugar and salt will dissolve. Sand will not dissolve.

Page 25: If you rub the design, you will feel the salt grains on the paper. If you rub the salt hard, most of it will come off the paper – but there will usually still be enough to show up faintly when you rub a soft pencil over it. The grains of salt catch on the soft graphite, and a dark pattern shows up. A hard pencil might not work well, because it rubs the salt on the surface of the paper away and the pattern will not show up clearly.

Page 29: The egg remains if you pour the vinegar away but, instead of a shell, it has a thick, white skin. The experiment also works if you use a hard-boiled egg – but the egg tastes horrible – don't even try to eat it.

Index

Further information

http://ksnn.larc.nasa.gov/k2/s_statesMatter.html
About materials – solids, gases and liquids.

www.bbc.co.uk/schools/ks2bitesize/science/
materials.shtml
About materials – for children aged 7 to 11.

www.primaryresources.co.uk/science/
science3a.htm
Links to a whole range of resources on the
subject of materials.

www.whocaresonline.org/assetbank/learning_
centre/letts/Courses/ks2_Science/ks2_0_sc.html
An informative interactive site.

www.sciencetech.technomuses.ca/english/school
zone/materials.cfm
A site attached to the Canadian Science and
Technology Museum, in Ottawa.

www.classzone.com/books/earth_science/terc/
content/visualizations/es1405/es1405page01.cf
m?chapter_no=visualization
An animation about how a cave forms.